My Feelings

WHEN I FEEL
JEALOUS

Amy Beattie

E **Enslow Publishing**
101 W. 23rd Street
Suite 240
New York, NY 10011
USA

enslow.com

Published in 2020 by Enslow Publishing, LLC
101 W. 23rd Street, Suite 240, New York, NY 10011

Copyright © 2020 by Enslow Publishing, LLC.

Library of Congress Cataloging-in-Publication Data

Names: Beattie, Amy, author.
Title: When I feel jealous / Amy Beattie.
Description: New York, NY : Enslow Publishing, LLC, 2020. | Series: My
 feelings | Includes bibliographical references and index. | Audience: Grades 1–2.
Identifiers: LCCN 2019009314| ISBN 9781978511705 (library bound) | ISBN
 9781978511675 (pbk.) | ISBN 9781978511682 (6 pack)
Subjects: LCSH: Jealousy in children—Juvenile literature. |
 Jealousy—Juvenile literature. | Envy—Juvenile literature.
Classification: LCC BF723.J4 B43 2020 | DDC 155.5/1248—dc23
LC record available at https://lccn.loc.gov/2019009314

Printed in the United States of America

To Our Readers: We have done our best to make sure all websites in this book were active and appropriate when we went to press. However, the author and the publisher have no control over and assume no liability for the material available on those websites or on any websites they may link to. Any comments or suggestions can be sent by email to customerservice@enslow.com.

Photo Credits: Cover KatsiarynaKa2/Shutterstock.com; cover, p. 1 (emoji) Cosmic_Design/Shutterstock.com; pp. 4, 5 Polka Dot Images/Getty Images; pp. 6, 7 Sergey Nivens/Shutterstock.com; pp. 8, 9, 10, 11, 22, 23 JGI/Jamie Grill /Getty Images; pp. 12, 14, 15 Kinzie Riehm/Image Source/Getty Images; p. 13 Sergey Novikov/Shutterstock.com; pp. 16, 17 Donald Iain Smith/Moment/Getty Images; pp. 18, 21 Tetra Images/Getty Images; p. 19 wavebreakmedia /Shutterstock.com; p. 20 Tetra Images/Brand X Pictures/Getty Images.

Contents

New Bike..4

Art Class 6

Baby Brother 8

Recess 12

Beach Vacation 16

Different Strengths 18

Being Jealous 22

Words to Know 24

Index 24

I feel jealous when my friend gets a new bike. It is faster than my bike. I wish I had a fast bike.

I ask my friend if I can **borrow** it one day. She says yes. I will share my toys with her, too.

I feel jealous when I do not get crayons in art class. I do not like painting.

My teacher says there will be more crayons
next week. I have to wait until then.

I feel jealous when my mommy plays with my baby brother. I want her to play with me.

Mommy says not to be mean to him. He is little. He needs help. She helped me when I was a baby, too.

Mommy says she and I can spend time together every Saturday. I get to choose what we do!

I wish Mommy and I could do fun things every day. When my brother gets bigger, all of us will have fun together.

I feel jealous when my friends play at recess without me. I hate playing tag!

I want to shout at them. My teacher says that will not help. It is okay if sometimes they play a game I do not like.

She tells me to go to the playground. It is nice to play with different kids sometimes.

I like trying new things. Tomorrow I will ask my friends if they want to play on the playground.

I feel jealous when our neighbors go on a big beach vacation.

My mom says she is jealous, too! I am glad we feel the same way. We have fun near home. We go to the **aquarium**.

I feel jealous when my big sister wins a prize at her school. I think I will never be as smart as she is.

My dad says every person has different **strengths**. My sister is good at school. What am I good at?

I am good at helping my dad build things. I am a good friend.

I am good at soccer. These things are important, too!

Lots of things make me feel jealous.

My friend shares with me. I will share with him and other people, too. Then we will feel less jealous.

Words to Know

aquarium A place to visit animals that live in the water.

borrow To use something that someone else has and then give it back.

strengths Things that people are good at.

Index

aquarium, 17
art class, 6
baby, 8–9
bike, 4–5
borrow, 5
brother, 8–9, 11
crayons, 6–7
dad, 20

friend, 4–5, 12, 15, 20, 23
mommy/mom, 8–11, 17
play, 8, 12–15
playground, 14–15
recess, 12
school, 18, 19

sharing, 5, 23
sister, 18–19
soccer, 21
strengths, 19
teacher, 7, 13
vacation, 16